TASUNKA

SOUTH DAKOTA
STATE HISTORICAL SOCIETY PRESS
PIERRE

TASUNKA

A Lakota Horse Legend

TOLD AND ILLUSTRATED BY Donald F. Montileaux

LAKOTA TRANSLATION BY AGNES GAY

This publication is funded, in part, by the Harold S. Shunk Memorial Fund and Dakota Authors, Inc.

Library of Congress Cataloging-in-Publication Data
Montileaux, Donald F., 1948-
Tasunka : a Lakota horse legend / told and illustrated by Donald F. Montileaux;
Lakota translation by Agnes Gay.—First edition.
pages cm
ISBN 978-0-9852905-2-8 (alk. paper)
1. Teton mythology. 2. Creation—Mythology. I. Title.
E99.T34M66 2014
978.004'975244—dc23
2013027799

The paper in this book meets the guidelines for permanence and durability
of the committee on Production Guidelines for Book Longevity
of the Council on Library Resources.

Text and cover design by Lydia D'moch

Please visit our website at www.sdshspress.com

Printed in China

Production date November 2013
Plant & location Printed by Everbest Printing (Guangzhou, China), Co. Ltd.
Job/Batch# 116461

18 17 16 15 14   1 2 3 4 5

For Alex White Plume
and all Lakota storytellers and elders

INTRODUCTION

The people of the plains had the horse for centuries,
and all one has to do to realize this is to walk into any
prehistoric museum and look at the three-toed horse.

—ALEX WHITE PLUME, LAKOTA STORYTELLER

Storytellers are tribal people who keep the history of ancient lifetimes. They use wisdom and gifted voices to teach young people. The storytellers paint pictures of wonderful, magical animals and colorful birds on the walls of their young minds.

Now, I have entered this arena of oral tradition to pass on the history and stories that I know. This history is important because it helps us know where we come from. These stories also preserve the truths and myths of our ancestors.

Listening to elders inspired me to write down and illustrate the traditional stories for all those children whose eyes dance in the firelight. I wanted to create words and images that jump boldly from the pages and into their imaginations.

In this goal, I was inspired by Alex White Plume, a treasured storyteller and elder of the Lakota people. I spent five days on his ranch on the Pine Ridge Indian Reservation in South Dakota with twenty other people. We rode Indian ponies and lived in the old style, eating traditional foods and spending nights in tipis. We listened as Alex and others shared their stories around an evening fire. They spoke to us in the educational way of our forefathers, the Lakota people. These events inspired me to write this story, which is only one among the many legends of our people.

Although I had heard this story from others in my lifetime, the experience at the White Plume ranch was the one that inspired me to write it down on paper and begin to draw. I felt the time was proper.

I dedicate this to Alex White Plume and all the Lakota storytellers and elders who make firelight twinkle in children's eyes.

When Mother Earth was young, all things on her surface were learning their place.

One day a young warrior of the plains was hunting for game to feed his family, but game was hard to find. The winter had been long, and there were few animals in the area close to camp. The young man searched far from home to find new places to hunt.

Unci Maka teca hehan, taku akan he ki iyuha tanyan aye.

Unpetu wan el Zuya Wicasa teca wan oblaye etanhan ca wakul omani hecel tiwahe tawa ki wowicaku kte ayes iyeyin kte ki otehike. Waniyetu ki hanske na wicoti ikiyela wamakaskan conalapi. Koskalaka ki ti etan tehan wakul ole i.

He came to a stream in a wooded area and knelt down
to quench his thirst. A sharp noise made him lift his head.
Out of the corner of his eye, he glimpsed movement and
a flash of color. He froze and used all his skills as a hunter
to sense this new game. But he was too slow. Quiet had
returned to the woods.

Can oju wan el wakpa wan han ca el hi na cankpe akan
mni yatkin kte han taku nahun ca pakasin. Ista ihanke etan
taku skanskan wan oowa ca wayanke. Owanjila hingle
nahan wakul wopika ki iyuha un taku ki ablese wacin.
Ayas, lila hanhi. Can oju ki hektakiya inila he.

The hunter walked toward the place where he had seen something move and found tracks in the earth. They were unlike any he knew.

Curious and needing to find food for his family, he followed the trail.

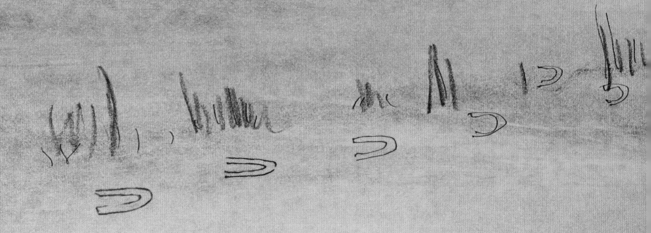

Wakul wicasa ki taku skanskan wayanke wan he ecetkiya mani ye na maka el owe ya iyeye. Tohani lececa wayanke sni.

Taku ki slolya cin nahan tiwahe tawa ki woyute wicakicin ca owe hena ihakab ye.

For days he tracked the unseen animal, if animal it even was. About ready to give up, he felt the ground rumble.

Unpetu tona wamakaskan wayanke sni he ole, wamakaskan heci. Wana ayustan kte han, maka ki nahunhunze.

Hundreds of beasts with fire surrounding their heads
and flowing from their bodies thundered past him.
The whole herd was as swift as the wind.

Wamakaskan opawange tona nata ohomni na
tacan ki etantan ileya buyela opta iyayapi. Optaye ki
ata tate se luzahanpi.

He ran after them, but the animals were faster than he was.
He fell farther and farther behind.

Wicakuwa ayas wamakaskan ki isamya ohankopi, samyes
unyan iyayapi.

As he cleared the top of a ridge, he suddenly dropped flat onto the ground. The herd had stopped to drink from a stream just ahead of him. All the beasts shimmered in the sun in colors he had never seen before. Red, blue, yellow, and green flowed along their necks and tails.

Paha aliya wakata i han ognahela kul blaskayela hinhpayeiciye. Itokab wakpa wan el optayela mniyatkan najinpi. Wamakaskan ki iyuha maste un wiyakpakpapi oowa ki le tohani wayanke sni. Tahu na sinte ognagna sa na to na zi nahan tozipi.

Their beauty dazzled the young warrior. He followed them for weeks across the plains. He learned their movements and habits. He wanted to catch one so that he could travel as fast as the wind.

Zuya wicasa ki owanyang wastepi un iyosnije. Oblaye opta oko tona wicihakob un. Tokeske oskinciyapi na ayapi ki hena unspeiciciye. Wanji oyuspa cin hecel tate se ohankoya omani kte.

At last, he found himself close to one of the younger animals. The warrior talked to the pony in a quiet voice and rubbed its flank.

The pony allowed the young man onto his back, and together they learned to cover the miles quickly.

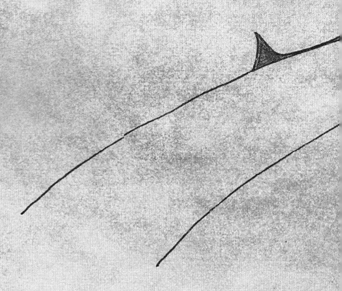

Kitanhci wamakaskan teca wan el kiyela i. Zuya wicasa ki ho niskala un wokiyake nahan oyute ki pawinte. Sunkcikala ki koskala he cuwe el akan yake kiye na numpi makiyutapi ki ohankoya i unspeiciciyapi.

The young man trained other horses until one day he noticed that the sun's heat was weaker and the nights were becoming cold. His time away from his tribe and family had grown too long.

He gathered his mounts and journeyed home.

Koskalaka ki uma sunkawakan ko wicakaunspe ecel anpetu wan el taku ableze, wi ki hehan kate sni na hunhepi ki osni aye. Ehas oyate tawa na tiwahe tawa etan lila tehan un.

Sunkawakan ki ptayela iwicakikcu na tiyatakiya kigle.

He whooped as he got close to his camp, and family members ran from the tipis to greet him. They stopped in fear as they saw his new companions. Young and old watched with wide eyes and fearful murmurs as the warrior rode into camp with his small herd of colorful ponies.

Ti kiyela gle hun akisasa, tiwahe umpi hena tipi etantan iyuskinya iyankapi. Kicica hena wawicayankapi na kowicakpapi ca inajinpi. Teca na kan ki wawicayankapi na ista niskaska un kokipapi ca el iglepi. Ecun, zuya wicasa ki he sunkawakan hin totokca optaye cikala tawa ki ob ti el glihuni.

The young man showed his people how to touch the animals and then to ride them.

The tribe began to hunt and travel farther than they had before. They had no trouble finding game. Soon they had plenty to eat and new clothes to wear. The tribe became wealthy and strong.

Koskala he ta oyate ki toske wamakaskan hena
ewicapatanpi na akan wicayakapi kte ki wicakipazo.
Oyate ki itokab tohani hehan tehan wakul ipi sni.
Wamakaskan ki oicu wastepi. Ecani woyute ota
yuhapi na hayapi lecala umpi. Oyate ki jicapi
na wasakapi.

They took pride in their new-found strength.
They started pushing other tribes out of their path.
They claimed lands that before had been used
by everyone.
    All who stood in their way were driven out.

Wowasake iyeyab he un wowitan
yuhapi. Oyate uma ki pahayab iyewicayapi,
makoce iyuha ehani umpi hena tawa iciyapi.
Tuwa kuseya najinpi hena wicakisicapi.

The Great Spirit looked on in sadness.

Tasunka, the horse, had been his gift to all the people. Instead, one tribe was abusing the gift. They were growing wealthy while others were going hungry, so the Great Spirit took the gift away.

Wakan Tanka wawicayanke na iyoksice.

Tasunka he oyate ki iyuha wicaku. Ecanyes oyate wanji wawicakupi he un sicaya kuwapi. Hena jica ayapi na kohan uma hena ins locinpi ca Wakan Tanka wawicaku he ikikcu.

Once again all people were the same, walking the earth and finding life hard. They missed Tasunka.

Ca ake oyate ki iyuha hektakiya unpi, maka manipi na wiconi ki otehike iyeyapi. Tasunka kiksuyapi.

Many centuries passed. The elders told the story of
Tasunka to the children of the tribe. As they grew up,
they remembered the gift of the Great Spirit, but they also
knew that the horse had been taken away because they
had used it to hurt others.

Omaka opawange ota iyaye. Wakan ki Tasunka
wicooyake he oyate etan wakanyeja ki owicakiyakapi.
Icagyapi ecel Wakan Tanka wawicaku wan he kiksuyapi
na le nakun slolyapi sunkawakan ki un oyate uma ki ksuye
wicayapi ca heun hena wicakipi.

One day a warrior was out hunting. He saw a bright light twinkling in the distance.

Anpetu wan el Zuya Wicasa wan wakul un. Kaiyuzeyata iyoyunpa wan ilehlega ca wayanke.

He worked his way closer and discovered a strange man riding an animal he had never seen before. The warrior remembered the stories of his elders and knew that the animal must be Tasunka, the horse.

Yin na kanyela i yunkan wicasa tokeca wan wamakaskan wan tohani wayanke sni ca akan yake ca ableze. Zuya Wicasa ki ehanni wicooyake ya wakan ki oyakapi hena kiksuye na he wamakaskan ki Tasunka wan he e seca ca slolye.

In the years that followed, more strangers passed through the land. These newcomers brought many horses with them. Soon the tribes had horses once again.

Waniyetu tona he ohakab oyate tokeca sunm ota makoce ki
opta iyayapi. Oyate lecala ki lena sunkawakan ota awicahipi.
Ecanni oyate ki ake sunkawakan wicayuhapi.

The return of Tasunka to the plains people was the Great Spirit's way of forgiveness. The people of the plains became wealthy as the horse reentered their camps, and great horsemen rode the plains once again.

Lakota Oyate ki Wakan Tanka awicakiciktunja ca he un sunkawakan ki glipi. Sunkawakan ki ake wicoti el glipi na ake wicasa sungwopika hena oblaye tanka ki ata sunkakan yanka omanipi.

A Note about the Illustrations

These illustrations are like the drawings that can be found in old ledger books. Traders and government agents used ledger books to keep records. These books date from 1860 to 1910, a period when American Indians were trading with white people and learning to use new drawing materials. I have studied ledger drawings for many years, and my art follows these simple forms that can tell complex stories.

FURTHER READING

First People of America and Canada. *Native American Legends.*
  http://www.firstpeople.us/FP-Html-Legends/Legends-AB.html.

Goble, Paul. *The Man Who Dreamed of Elk Dogs & Other Stories from the Tipi.*
  Bloomington, Ind.: Wisdom Tales, 2012.

Montileaux, Donald F. *Tatanka and the Lakota People: A Creation Story.* Pierre:
  South Dakota State Historical Society Press, 2006.